Walt Disney's DONALD DUCK

•• THE CRITIC ••

Later—

JUST IMAGINE, BOYS, I'LL BE IN THE BIG BUCKS AND WELL KNOWN! A REGULAR MAN ABOUT TOWN AND PURVEYOR OF BONS MOTS GALORE!

YEAH? BUT WHAT DO YOU KNOW ABOUT **ART**?

WHAT'S TO KNOW? I'VE GOT EYES, HAVEN'T I?

YOU'VE GOT ARMS AND LEGS, TOO, BUT YOU'VE NEVER CLIMBED **MOUNT EVEREST!**

FAUGH! A NON-SEQUITUR IF EVER I HEARD ONE!

BESIDES, I'LL HAVE YOU GUYS KNOW THAT WHEN I WAS IN THE THIRD GRADE MY PAINTING OF AN ONION WAS THE **BEST IN THE CLASS!**

DID ANYONE **ELSE** PAINT AN ONION?

NEVER MIND! NOW THAT I'M A CENTRAL FIGURE IN DUCKBURG'S ART WORLD, MY MIND HAS RISEN ABOVE SUCH MUNDANE CONCERNS!

TALK ABOUT NON-SEQUITURS!

And so—

OFF YOU GO, DUCK! THE GALLERY IS AT 337 73RD AVENUE! DEADLINE IS TWO O'CLOCK, SO HOP TO IT!

YES **SIR!** ON MY WAY!

OH BOY! MY FIRST SHOW! LET'S SEE, SHALL I USE RAPIER WIT, OR DO A HOMESPUN APPROACH FOR MY REVIEW?

DAILY BLA

HMM! WHAT **WAS** THAT ADDRESS? 373 73ᴿᴰ AVENUE? NO, THAT'S NOT RIGHT! AH, I KNOW, IT WAS 373 **37ᵀᴴ AVENUE!**

SOON—

ODD LOOKING ART GALLERY! LOOKS MORE LIKE A JUNK-YARD! OH WELL, SOMETIMES IT'S HARD TO TELL THE DIFFERENCE NOWADAYS!

WHAT'S THAT YOU SAY, BUD?

I SAID THAT I'M AMUSED BY THE PRESUMPTION OF YOUR **CHIAROSCURO!**

SOONER YET—

OW! I GUESS I'D BETTER CALL IN AND CHECK THAT ADDRESS AGAIN!

BONK

AND SOON AGAIN—

INTERESTING! TELL ME, SIR, WAS ANYBODY **HURT?**

HURT? WHY? WHAT ARE YOU TALKING ABOUT?

YOU KNOW, WHEN THE PAINT FACTORY BLEW UP!

I **BEG** YOUR PARDON?

WELL **HOW ELSE** COULD A MESS LIKE THAT HAPPEN?

LATER, BACK AT THE OFFICE—

DO YOU USUALLY STAND UP WHEN YOU TYPE, DUCK?

ONLY WHEN IT HURTS TO **SIT!**

MORNING!

WELL, WHAT DO YOU THINK OF MY FIRST REVIEW?

YOU BETTER HOPE THE ARTIST IS LIVING ON THE **MOON!**

ARTIST MY FOOT! I COULD DO BETTER PAINTINGS THAN THOSE IN MY SLEEP!

MAYBE, MAYBE NOT!

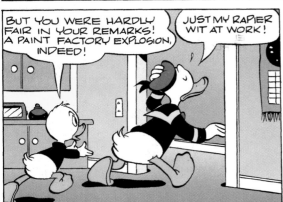

BUT YOU WERE HARDLY FAIR IN YOUR REMARKS! A PAINT FACTORY EXPLOSION, INDEED!

JUST MY RAPIER WIT AT WORK!

AT ANY RATE I'M OFF ON ANOTHER JOB! THIS TIME I'LL TRY TO BE MORE **FOLKSY!**

THUS—

SO YOU'RE THE ARTIST, HUH? YUK! YUK! MAN ALIVE, THESE HERE DO-DADS IS SURE GOT THEIR AMUSIN' MOMENTS!

YOU DON'T SAY!

SURE DO! HAD A PLUMBER ONE TIME GOT THE PIPES ALL MESSED UP THIS-A-WAY! HECK THUNDER! WE DIDN'T HAVE NO WATER IN THE HOUSE FER A WHOLE **WEEK!** YUK! YUK!

DID YOU SAY YOU'RE AN **ART CRITIC**?

YOU BET YER MAMMY'S SOUP I AM! GOT ME AN ARTY EYE LIKE A HAWK, TOO! I KIN SEE RIGHT THROUGH ALL THIS HERE KINDA JUNK EASY AS PIE!

MERE MINUTES LATER—

WELL, SO MUCH FOR FOLKSY! WHEN I GET THROUGH WITH THAT THUG HE'LL BE SELLING DOORKNOBS ON EASTER ISLAND!

With each passing day Donald manages to increase the ire of Duckburg's art world!

I WOULD VENTURE TO SAY THAT THE HORIZONTAL OBJECTIVITY HERE IS MORE THAN OFFSET BY THE DELICATE BALANCE OF VERTICAL PLATITUDE!

MEANING?

THIS STUFF STINKS!

BUT DON'T WORRY, YOU CAN READ ALL ABOUT IT IN MORE DETAIL IN TOMORROW'S DAILY BLA! TA! TA!

Before long, it is Donald himself who becomes the object of critique!

YOU THE GUY WOT TRASHED MY SHOW OF DELICATE PAINTIN'S OF FLOWER COVERED ANVILS?

YOU MIGHT SAY THAT!

YEAH, AN' I MIGHT ALSO KNUCKLE UP YER NOODLE, GET ME?

OH NO YOU DON'T! HE'S MINE! HE DUMPED ON MY EXHIBIT OF PORCELAIN FOOTBALL HELMETS!

WHAT ABOUT ME? THIS TIN-HORN HACK TORPEDOED THE SHOWING OF MY LATEST MASTERPIECE! A TWELVE FOOT LONG AMOEBA MADE FROM TOOTHPICKS!

MAYBE WE OUGHTA RUN HIM OUTTA TOWN!

OR TAR AND FEATHER HIM!

JUST THE TAR! HE'S ALREADY COVERED WITH FEATHERS!

C AUGHT! DONALD HAS NO GRACEFUL WAY OUT! SO —

SIGH! I SUPPOSE EVEN REMBRANDT HAD HIS BAD MOMENTS!

HOWEVER, THE TRUE ARTIST NEVER LETS SMALL MISHAPS MAR HIS LASER-LIKE CONCENTRATION!

AH, THE FLOWER AND THE FOOTBALL! A BEAUTIFUL METAPHOR FOR SOMETHING OR OTHER!

HMM! I CAN'T SEEM TO GET THE FOOTBALL RIGHT! IT LOOKS MORE LIKE A LEATHER **WATERMELON**!

I WONDER IF **THAT** COULD BE A METAPHOR FOR ANYTHING?

OH, WELL . . .

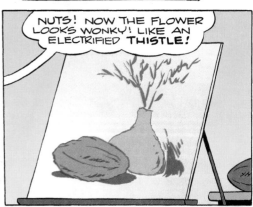

NUTS! NOW THE FLOWER LOOKS WONKY! LIKE AN ELECTRIFIED **THISTLE**!

PHOOEY! THE HECK WITH STILL LIFES! MAYBE I SHOULD PAINT FROM THE **MINDSCAPE**! LET MY IMAGINATION **FLOW**!

NOW IT'S COMING! A SYMBOLIC **SELF** PORTRAIT!

HOW'S IT COMING, LAUTREC?

LIMNED ANYTHING SIGNIFICANT?

ME, I THINK!

YOU? WELL, MAYBE! THAT IS, AS LONG AS YOU SEE YOURSELF AS A **MUSHROOM WITH WARTS!**

IT'S ONLY SUPPOSED TO BE **SYMBOLIC**, FOR CRYIN' OUT LOUD!

IT **IS**! IT'S SYMBOLIC OF A MUSHROOM WITH WARTS!

THAT'S IT! **I GIVE UP!**

SPLAT

EVERYBODY'S A CRITIC!

EVEN YOU!

MAKE THAT **WAS**! I'M GOING TO GO SULK AND KISS MY JOB AS AN ART CRITIC **GOODBYE!**

POOR UNCA DONALD! HE ALWAYS BITES OFF MORE THAN HE CAN CHEW!

AND THEN CAN'T FOLLOW THROUGH!

HEY! I WONDER! AFTER ALL, HE DID **TRY**, DIDN'T HE? THAT'S GOT TO COUNT FOR **SOMETHING!**

SO?

SO WHY DON'T WE GO AHEAD AND ENTER HIS PAINTING IN THE COMPETITION?

ARE YOU KIDDING? **THAT THING**?

WHY NOT? IT CAN'T BE MUCH WORSE THAN THE REST OF THE STUFF THAT'S ENTERED!

YEAH, AND IF NOTHING ELSE, IT'LL SHOW **COURAGE**!

YOU CAN SAY **THAT** AGAIN!

DONALD'S PAINTING IS DULY ENTERED, AND LO, WHEN THE JUDGING IS COMPLETE—

I'M PROUD TO ANNOUNCE, LADIES AND GENTLEMEN, THAT THE FIRST PRIZE GOES TO THE ESTEEMED ART CRITIC OF THE DAILY BLA...

... MISTER DONALD DUCK, FOR HIS WONDERFULLY EVOCATIVE PAINTING, "SYMPHONY IN FUNGUS"!

CLAP CLAP CLAP

LATER, BUT NOT MUCH—

AS YOU CAN NO DOUBT DISCERN, THE CHIAROSCURO OF THE DIAGONAL IS THE LINCHPIN OF THE TANGENTIAL ELEMENTS THAT WELD CONCEPT WITH BELIEF...

MARVELOUS, MISTER DUCK! TELL US **MORE**!

O.P.U. T.V.

WALT DISNEY'S
MICKEY MOUSE

JOINS THE FOREIGN LEGION!

Q: WHY DID THE SECRET SERVICEMAN JOIN THE LEGION?

A: TO EXPOSE CROOKED SERGEANT PEGLEG PETE AND HIS ACCOMPLICE, TRIGGER HAWKES!

HAWKES STOLE SOME GUN BLUEPRINTS FROM THE SECRET SERVICE! PRIVATE MICKEY FINDS THEM HIDDEN IN PETE'S OFFICE...

...BUT PETE GETS THE DROP ON HIM, AND MICKEY IS FOILED!

WE'RE GONNA CARRY THESE BLUEPRINTS WITH US FROM NOW ON!

THE TWO VILLAINS PLAN TO DESERT MICKEY'S SQUAD AT SIKH ABED OASIS! THEN PETE'S LOCAL ALLY, BANDIT CHIEF YUSSUF AIPER, WILL *RUB THEM ALL OUT!*

THAT'LL GIVE US PLENTY OF TIME TO GET AWAY WITH TH' GUN PLANS — 'CUZ WE'LL BE REPORTED KILLED WITH TH' REST OF TH' PARTY!

BUT WE CAN'T ARREST THEM JUST ON SUSPICION! AFTER ALL, THEY HAVEN'T ACTUALLY **DONE** ANYTHING YET!

I'LL TELL YA WHAT WE CAN DO, SIR! LISTEN!

UNDER THE COLONEL'S AUTHORITY, MICKEY ORDERS A VAST WEAPONS SHIPMENT FROM THE ARMORY!

THEN, POSING AS A MERCHANT, HE SELLS THE WHOLE LOT TO AIPER AND HIS CLAN!

THE BUSINESS DEAL IS COMPLETED! YUSSUF AIPER'S OLD RIFLES ARE LOADED ON MICKEY'S CARAVAN, AND AIPER'S MEN ARE NOW EQUIPPED WITH NEW ONES!

I AM VERY HAPPY! FOR YEARS, I HAVE BEEN CALLED THE "SCOURGE OF THE DESERT!" NOW I CAN BECOME ITS KING!

I WILL LOOT AND PLUNDER AND PILLAGE UNTIL THE DESERT FLOWS RED, AND PEOPLE TREMBLE WHEN THEY HEAR MY NAME!

AND ALL BECAUSE YOU SOLD ME THESE RIFLES! IT WAS A GREAT FAVOR! I WILL NEVER FORGET IT! AND NOW, MY FRIEND— BEFORE WE PART—

I'LL TAKE BACK THAT THREE THOUSAND DOLLARS I PAID YOU!

HAVING EXCHANGED HIS OLD RIFLES FOR MICKEY'S NEW ONES, YUSSUF AIPER DEMANDS THAT THE MONEY HE PAID BE RETURNED!

WHY—WHY— YOU BIG—!

LET'S NOT ARGUE ABOUT IT— OR I MAY CHANGE MY MIND AND KILL YOU, AFTER ALL!

I AM GLAD YOU ARE WISE AS WELL AS SHREWD! FAREWELL, MY FRIEND! MY GOOD FORTUNE ATTEND YOU!

THE BIG DOUBLE-CROSSING, CROOKED, MURDERING CHISELER!

YEAH! HE SURE IS!

AN' HE DOESN'T KNOW IT— BUT HE'S ALSO AN AWFUL SUCKER!

IT'S MIDNIGHT, LIEUTENANT MOUSE!

GOOD! AWAKEN TH' MEN! STATION 'EM IN A BIG CIRCLE AROUND CAMP— FIFTY YARDS APART! AN' TELL 'EM T' KEEP OUT O' SIGHT!

AN' NO FIRING— UNLESS I GIVE TH' COMMAND! UNDERSTAND? NO MATTER WHAT HAPPENS— NOT A SINGLE SHOT FROM ANYBODY!

BUT— BUT, LIEUTENANT! IT IS SUICIDE! WE WILL BE SLAUGHTERED!

LISTEN, CORPORAL! IT'S A CINCH WE'LL BE SLAUGHTERED IF WE FIGHT 'EM! THEY OUTNUMBER US TEN TO ONE! TH' ONLY WAY WE CAN LICK 'EM IS BY STRATEGY!

AN' THOSE BIRDS ARE GONNA RIDE SMACK INTO THE DOGGONEDEST BIGGEST MESS O' STRATEGY THAT EVER HIT TH' DESERT!

Y-Y-YES, SIR!

GET GOIN'!

THE COLD, BREATHLESS HOURS BEFORE DAWN! MICKEY'S MEN LIE FIFTY YARDS APART, IN A HUGE CIRCLE—

HUSHED— FEARFUL— MOTIONLESS—

WAITING FOR THE ATTACK THEY KNOW IS COMING!

BOY! THIS IS SURE TOUGH ON A GUY'S NERVES! AN' IF JUST ONE MAN BREAKS UNDER IT— WE'RE SUNK!

BUT THEY'RE GOOD MEN— AN' GOOD SOLDIERS! AN' THEY KNOW HOW TO OBEY ORDERS!

THEN— SUDDENLY— THE AIR IS SPLIT BY BLOOD-CURDLING SHRIEKS— AND THE BEAT OF A THOUSAND HOOFS!

CHARGE!

AND DON'T LET A SINGLE MAN ESCAPE!

WITH YUSSUF AIPER'S BAND DISARMED AND THE WAR DEPARTMENT'S STOLEN GUN PLANS ALMOST IN HIS GRASP, MICKEY MAKES A STARTLING DISCOVERY: **PEGLEG PETE HAS DISAPPEARED!**

HE WAS RIGHT BESIDE ME WHEN WE REACHED THE CAMP!

BUT WHERE COULD HE HAVE GONE? WHO SAW HIM LAST?

I DID! WHILE THE BAND WAS WRECKING THE CAMP, HE SLIPPED AWAY AND RODE ACROSS THE DESERT! HE PASSED NOT TWENTY FEET FROM ME!

WELL, FOR TH' LOVE O' MIKE— WHY DIDN'T YA **STOP** 'IM?

I COULDN'T, LIEUTENANT!

YOU SAID — NO MATTER WHAT HAPPENED — NOBODY WAS TO FIRE UNTIL YOU GAVE THE COMMAND! I JUST OBEYED ORDERS, SIR!

HAVING RISKED HIS LIFE TO RECOVER THE STOLEN BLUEPRINTS, AND ALMOST HAVING THEM IN HIS GRASP, MICKEY FINDS THAT PETE HAS SLIPPED THROUGH THE TRAP— AND ESCAPED!

DOGGONE TH' COCKEYED LUCK! ALL MY HARD WORK FOR NUTHIN'! HE GOT AWAY AS CLEAN AS A WHISTLE!

THE DOUBLE— CROSSING APE!

BUT I'D FEEL A LOT WORSE IF HE'D HAD THOSE BLUEPRINTS WITH HIM!

WHAT???

YA MEAN —HE HASN'T **GOT** 'EM?

YOU THINK I'D LET THAT DOUBLE-CROSSER CARRY 'EM? NOT A CHANCE! I STOLE 'EM FROM HIM IN THE BANDITS' CAMP!

HERE YOU ARE! I HOPE THEY'LL DO **YOU** MORE GOOD THAN THEY DID **ME!**

MICKEY'S LONG SEARCH FOR THE STOLEN WAR DEPARTMENT GUN PLANS HAS ENDED!

AT LAST, HE HAS THEM IN HIS HANDS!

LIEUTENANT MOUSE, SIR! THE COLONEL HAS JUST ARRIVED — WITH A DETACHMENT OF SOLDIERS!

HOT DIGGETTY! THAT IS — TELL HIM I'LL REPORT AT ONCE!

YOU COME WITH ME, TRIGGER! I'M KEEPIN' MY EYES ON YA, FROM NOW ON!

WHAT'S THE LEGION GONNA DO WITH ME, MICKEY? SHOOT ME AS A DESERTER?

NOT A CHANCE! I'M TAKIN' YA BACK HOME! AFTER THAT, IT'S UP TO TH' DEPARTMENT O' JUSTICE!

I GUESS THIS JUST ADDS ANOTHER CHAPTER TO THE OLD STORY: CRIME DOESN'T PAY!

WELL — MEBBE NOT A WHOLE CHAPTER! BUT I CAN GUARANTEE IT'LL ADD AT LEAST A SENTENCE!

LIEUTENANT MOUSE, REPORTING TO THE COLONEL, SIR! YOUR ASSIGNMENT HAS BEEN COMPLETED!

YUSSUF AIPER AN' HIS BAND ARE DISARMED! I RECOVERED TH' PAPERS I WAS AFTER — AN' CAPTURED TH' THIEF THAT STOLE 'EM!

ALL THERE IS LEFT T' DO IS SEND A DETACHMENT O' TROOPS TO AIPER'S CAMP — AN' PICK UP TH' REST O' TH' RIFLES AN' AMMUNITION!

CONGRATULATIONS, MY LAD! AND YOUR VICTORY WAS ACHIEVED WITHOUT A MAN ON EITHER SIDE BEING INJURED IN ANY WAY!

WELL — PRACTICALLY, SIR! BUT I'VE GOT A HUNCH THAT A COUPLE O' GUYS HAD THEIR **FEELINGS** HURT PRETTY BAD!

BACK IN DASSIS ALI! YUSSUF AIPER IS IN JAIL, AWAITING TRIAL!

WITHOUT A LEADER, HIS BAND HAS DISBANDED! AND MICKEY, HAVING OBTAINED HIS DISCHARGE, IS READY TO LEAVE FOR HOME!

GOOD-BYE, MY LAD! A GUARD OF HONOR WILL ACCOMPANY YOU AND YOUR PRISONER TO THE BOAT! ONCE ABOARD, YOU WILL HAVE NO TROUBLE!

AND IF YOU EVER WANT TO COME BACK— I WILL BE PROUD TO HAVE YOU AS AN OFFICER IN MY BATTALION!

THANK YA, SIR! AN YA CAN'T TELL— MEBBE SOME DAY I WILL!

BUT— BEFORE I GO— I WAN'T T' DO JUST ONE MORE THING!

WHAT IS THAT?

I WANT T' SALUTE TH' SWELLEST OFFICER TH' FOREIGN LEGION EVER HAD!

ACCOMPANIED BY A GUARD OF HONOR, MICKEY REACHES THE PORT OF AITA KLAH KURFU

AND TAKES TRIGGER HAWKES ABOARD SHIP!

CAPTAIN! THIS PRISONER IS TO BE PUT IN IRONS— AN' KEPT THERE!

IT SHALL BE DONE AT ONCE!

BOS'N! THROW THIS MAN IN THE BRIG! POST A SPECIAL GUARD OVER HIM— NIGHT AND DAY!

AYE, AYE, SIR!

THE SECRET SERVICE WILL HOLD YOU PERSONALLY RESPONSIBLE FOR HIM TILL WE REACH HOME!

DON'T WORRY, SIR! YOU CAN PUT YOUR MIND ABSOLUTELY AT REST!

AN'— WHAT'S MORE— THAT'S NOT ALL I'M GONNA PUT ABSOLUTELY AT REST FOR TH' NEXT WEEK OR SO!

TWO WEEKS LATER! AFTER A RESTFUL AND UNEVENTFUL VOYAGE, MICKEY'S SHIP DOCKS AT HOME! AND AS HE WALKS DOWN THE GANGPLANK—

CAPTAIN DOBERMAN!

MICKEY! HOW ARE YOU, BOY?

GOLLY, BUT I'M GLAD T'SEE YA! IT WAS SWELL OF YA T'COME DOWN AN' MEET ME!

SWELL OF ME! GREAT GRIEF! I'M PROUD TO MEET YOU! YOU'VE DONE A GRAND JOB, MY BOY — A MARVELOUS JOB!

PIER 128 SHIP LINES CO.

YOU KNOW, MICKEY— WE DIDN'T HEAR FROM YOU FOR SO LONG THAT WE'D JUST ABOUT GIVEN YOU UP!

I DON'T BLAME YA! FOR A WHILE, THERE, I WAS ABOUT TO GIVE MYSELF UP!

MAJOR BEAGLE CHIEF OF BUREAU OF INVESTIGATION

MAJOR BEAGLE, SIR!

MICKEY MOUSE! WELL, BLESS MY SOUL! I'M GLAD TO SEE YOU! HOW DID YOU DO IT?

I JUST OBEYED ORDERS, SIR! YA TOLD ME T'FIND TH' BLUEPRINTS AN' TH' GUY WHO STOLE 'EM — AN' BRING 'EM BOTH BACK, SO I DID!

THIS IS THE CASE CARD DESCRIBING THE ROBBERY! AND, THOUGH YOUR ADVENTURES WOULD PROBABLY FILL A BOOK, ALL I CAN WRITE HERE IS SIX WORDS—

BLUEPRINTS RECOVERED! PRISONER ARRESTED! CASE SOLVED!

WELL— AFTER ALL, SIR — WHAT MORE IS THERE T' SAY?

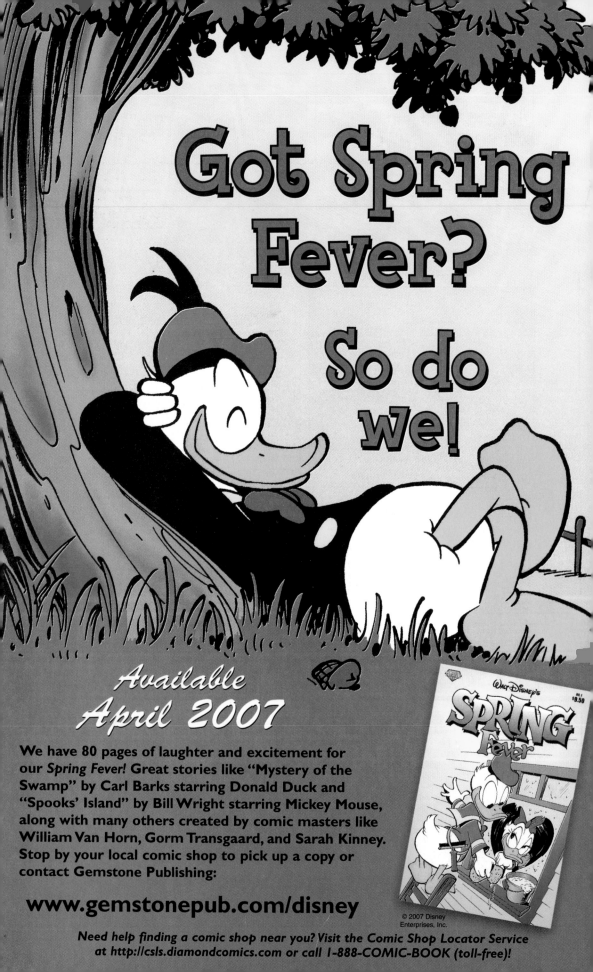

GOOFY in PRIMATE PASSION

Walt Disney's

PROFESSOR DUSTIBONES OF DRYUPP UNIVERSITY HAS ASKED MICKEY AND GOOFY TO DELIVER A VERY SPECIAL CARGO TO AN ISOLATED TROPICAL ISLAND—

GEE, GOOFY, WE'RE REALLY LUCKY TO HAVE BEEN SENT ON THIS MISSION!

I GUESS, MICKEY!

D 2001-086

YOU *GUESS?* I KNOW WE GOTTA GET THE PLANE BACK BY NIGHTFALL! BUT BEFORE THEN, WE GET ALL AFTERNOON TO *EXPLORE* THE *JUNGLE!*

≥SIGH!≤

WELL, I'M *BORED,* AN' IT'S DRIVIN' ME NUTS! I WANNA DO SOME EXPLORIN' RIGHT *NOW...*

NO PEEKING!

...BY JUST *LIFTING* THAT CLOTH A TEENY TINY BIT AND SEEIN' WHUT THUH *APE* LOOKS LIKE!

NO PEEKING!

≥SIGH!≤ I ONLY WISH WE COULD, GOOFY! BUT—

YEAH, I *KNOW!* THUH PROF SAID WE'RE NOT ALLOWED TO UNVEIL HER!

THE ONLY PEOPLE THE MONKEY'S EVER MET BEFORE ARE HER HANDLERS AT THE UNIVERSITY!

AND AS WE'RE TAKING HER TO MEET HER FUTURE MATE AT THE HABITAT, HER REACTION TO "NEW" FOLKS MIGHT *COMPLICATE* THINGS!

AW, COME ON, MICK! ONE LITTLE *PEEK* CAN'T HURT!

OKAY, GOOFY, YOU'VE PERSUADED ME! BESIDES I'M *CURIOUS*, TOO! LET'S SEE WHAT LOVEY LOOKS LIKE!

GAWRSH! SHE SEEMS FRIGHTENED, MICKEY!

TRY SAYING SOMETHING *NICE* TO REASSURE HER!

COME ON, LOVEY, YUH GORGEOUS GAL! WHY DON'T YOU GIVE ME A LOVELY SMILE? I'M SURE IT'S A *BEAUT*, SWEETUMS!

AREN'T YOU RATHER OVERDOING IT, GOOFY? DON'T GET TOO PASSIONATE! REMEMBER, SHE BELONGS TO SOME *OTHER* PRIMATE!

UMM... TELL THAT TUH *LOVEY!*

I THINK I OVERDID THE CHARM! AN' NOW I CAN'T *BREATHE!*

SMACK!

UH-OH! IF THAT'S THE REACTION HER HANDLERS WERE WORRIED ABOUT, THINGS MAY *REALLY* BE COMPLICATED NOW!

WELL, LOU IS DOING *GREAT* WHERE TREE-CLIMBING IS CONCERNED!

TRY NOT TO DO *WELL* ON THIS ONE, OKAY, GOOF?

SURE!

HOW'S THIS?

PERFECT! I MEAN... PERFECTLY *AWFUL!*

SN

WHOOOAA!

AWP! AAAAWP!

EEP! AWP!

AWP! EEP!

Hear Ye, Hear Ye!

Free Comic Book Day Cometh!

On the 5th Day of May in the Year 2007

Visit your local comic shop to pick up
your free Disney comic book featuring

Mickey Mouse
in
The Robin Hood Adventure

by Eisner Awards Hall of Fame Artist
Floyd Gottfredson

© 2007 Disney Enterprises, Inc.

GEMSTONE PUBLISHING

www.gemstonepub.com/disney

FETHRY! WHUT Y'ALL DOIN' HERE THAT A PIG COULDN'T DO BETTER?

YOU VARMINT...

...THAT A PIG COULDN'T...

...YER GETTIN' VENTILATED—

PIG! THAT'S IT! ≶GULP!≷ MOE, I'M HERE TO HELP GET A NEW PIG HERD FOR YOU!

IF THIS INVOLVES ANOTHER TRIP TA TH' CITY...

ONLY TO MAKE YOU FAMOUS AND WEALTHY, HARD HAID! THE PIGGIES WILL FOLLOW... NATURALLY!

CLONK!

MY RECORDER! MY TAPES!

GOTCHA!

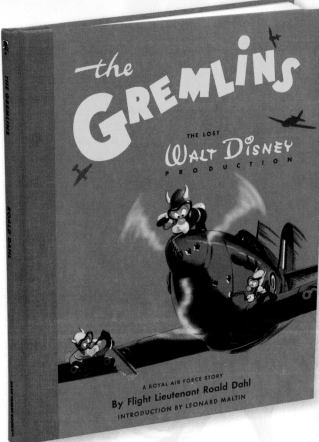

LOOKS LIKE UNCA DONALD'S MOVED ON TO "NATURE STUDIES"!

I HATE TO REPEAT MYSELF, BUT HE *REALLY IS GOOD!*

SO WHAT?! EVEN IF HE CARVED OUT PERFECT *ICE HAMBURGERS*, WE STILL COULDN'T *EAT* THEM!

YOU'VE GOT TO GET A *JOB* BEFORE WE ALL *STARVE*, UNCA DONALD! THERE'S NO *MONEY* IN SUCH *PERISHABLE* ART!

SHOWS WHAT *YOU* KNOW!

CHIP

IT JUST SO HAPPENS THAT DUCKBURG ICE INC. IS SPONSORING AN *ICE SCULPTING CONTEST*, AND THE FIRST PRIZE IS $1,000!

THIS IS JUST A *MOCK-UP* OF MY ENTRY! WITH *DAISY'S BEAUTY* AND MY *TALENT*, I'M A SHOO-IN TO WIN!

YOU WOULDN'T KNOW TALENT IF IT *BIT YOU* IN THE *BUTT*, DUCK!

SPLOOSH!

AND AS FAR AS YOUR GIRLFRIEND'S *BEAUTY* GOES, SHE LOOKS LIKE SHE BELONGS IN A CIRCUS *FREAKSHOW!* HAR HAR *HAR!*

IT'LL BE **YOU** WHO ENDS UP CRYING FOR HIS **MOMMY,** DUCK!

AND I'VE MADE **ANOTHER** ONE, JUST IN CASE YOU'RE NOT READY TO **SURRENDER!**

AND IT'LL BE **ME** WHO COMES OUT AHEAD IN THIS GAME!

CHONK!

WHOMP!

UNCA DONALD! MR. JONES! THIS HAS GONE **FAR ENOUGH!**

CAN'T YOU SETTLE WHO'S THE BETTER SCULPTOR AT THE **ICE SCULPTING CONTEST?**

THE BOYS ARE RIGHT! I'LL COME UP WITH A **NEW DESIGN** THAT WILL **STUN** THE JUDGES!

OH, YEAH? AFTER THEY SEE **MY** NEW DESIGN, THEY'LL BE SO **BLINDED** WITH IT'S BRILLIANCE THEY WON'T EVEN **LOOK** AT YOURS!

STILL, IT WON'T HURT TO BE **PREPARED** JUST IN CASE JONES GETS **LUCKY!**

STILL, IT WON'T HURT TO BE **PREPARED** JUST IN CASE DONALD GETS **LUCKY!**

YOU REALIZE THEY'LL END UP **DESTROYING** EACH OTHER'S SCULPTURES, DON'T YOU?

YEAH, WE'LL NEVER SEE A **PENNY** OF THAT PRIZE MONEY!

UNLESS **WE** ENTER THE CONTEST, TOO!

COMES THE DAY OF THE CONTEST –

LAST CALL FOR ENTRANTS! THE COMPETITION STARTS IN EXACTLY TEN MINUTES!

AT THAT POINT, EACH CONTESTANT WILL HAVE EXACTLY *ONE HOUR* TO FINISH THEIR SCULPTURE!

REMEMBER, THE SCULPTURE MUST BE *ENTIRELY* CARVED OUT OF THE SOLID BLOCK OF ICE PROVIDED BY DUCKBURG ICE, INC.! *NO ADD-ONS* ARE ALLOWED!

I'LL POLISH UP A THIN SLAB OF ICE SO IT'S A *MIRROR* THAT REFLECTS DAISY'S *BEAUTY!* THAT'S SURE TO *DOUBLE WOW* THE JUDGES!

HEH-HEH! IF THE JUDGES *ARE* WOWED BY *BEAUTY,* THIS BABE WILL *OUT-WOW* DONALD'S BEAKY GIRLFRIEND ANY DAY!

IT'S A GOOD THING THE JUDGES SAID WE COULD TOPPLE THE BLOCK OF ICE AND CARVE IT *HORIZONTALLY!*

YEAH, IT'D BE ALMOST *UNNATURAL* TO CARVE BORNWORTHY *SITTING UP!*

THE NEPHEWS ARE ALSO HAVING PROBLEMS WITH THEIR SCULPTURE —

~OOG!~ MAYBE THE JUDGES WILL THINK WE *WANTED* TO SCULPT A *MUTANT ALIEN SPACE DOG?*

BUT WHAT ABOUT GLADSTONE?

OH, MY! HAS MY LUCK *DESERTED* ME? OR HAS *CHANCE* IN FACT HANDED ME A *WINNING HAND?*

THE LATTER *MUST* BE TRUE! I'LL JUST HAVE TO TRUST TO *BLIND LUCK* AND...

CHINK!

CRACK!

WHUMP!

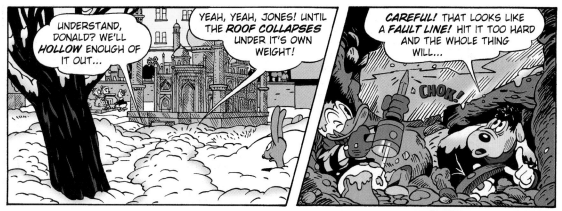